# Injuring Eternity

Cover design by Gineve Rudolph
Cover painting & photographs
by Charles Accardi

Mischievous Muse Press
A subsidiary of the
World Nouveau Company

Publisher ID: 6051514-10-9
ISBN: 978-0-9828865-4-0

Printed in the United States of America
10 9 8 7 6 5 4 3 2 1

Mischievous Muse Press
A Subsidiary of The World Nouveau Company
WWW.WORLDNOUVEAU.COM

As if you could kill time without injuring eternity.

-----Henry Thoreau

Thanks to my husband Charles for his loving support and inspiration and for the cover of this book; to my mother-in-love, Tana Accardi for all of her diligence and affection, to Robert Manaster for his incredible help with revisions and for being my writing pal for more years than I care to mention, to my best friend from across the pond Karen; my "Venice" friends Martha, Fawnathon, Dominic, Jeff, Pegarty, Melinda & Fortunado.

Special thanks to my teachers Dr. James Ragan and Dr. Gerald Locklin for their talent and their faith.

And a shout-out to the wonderful women in my writers group (WWW): Jean, Andrea, Bronwen, Nichole, Jennifer, Heather, Kathi, Georgia, Susan and Maja, without whose monthly get-togethers my creative fire would have extinguished; my long-distance writing buddies and fellow MPWers: Richie Rich, April, Ellen, and Tammy.

Also, thanks to the yoga teachers in Topanga for keeping me sane and upbeat and grateful (Hilary, Annmarie, Vivica, Matt) in the midst of this project.

And finally I am eternally grateful to all those who were called upon to provide references for me through the years—especially my friend Donna who has been writing recommendations for me since the late 1980s.

For my mother and father (who supported my creative efforts—even when they did not understand)

Audrey Markham Borges and Art Borges

# Injuring Eternity

## Millicent Borges Accardi

# Morning

# Noon

# Evening

T
A
B
L
E

O
F

C
O
N
T
E
N
T
S

# Morning

## His Hand on her Black Pants

For Jean and Rick

Because they were not parents
Yet, and it was one of their evenings
Out before the last Mother's Day
She was not a mother, he pictured what
Their lives would soon become, the calm
Before the storm, and she was herself
For one of the last times, holding on
To his fingers in a kind way because
He was named for Chopin and because
He had agreed to go to this concert. Her
Black pants and uncrossed legs
Against his white fingers were all
She could see of the piano keys.

## Mourning Doves

Have such soulful
Eyes, their gray suit
Of feathers blurs and sinks
Them into the background
Like a creature in hiding.
They hover below the wild
Bird feeder set up for finches
And harvest the shells, the thistle
Seed casings and what drops after
The finches and faux robins and phoebes
Have feasted. The mourning
Doves huddle and nest in the mountains
Of seed shells and dirt and make circles
With their small bird bodies turning
Into the ground digging a place around
Them as if they were under a shrub with only
The black drops of ink from their tail feathers
Visible. In a group, they lie in wait, their dear gray
Eyes gloomy and sullen and innocent and they want
What the world desires, to be fed and comfortable
And consummated and happy.

## Poor Little Sod

For Karen and Thomas Charles

My friend talks about her child
With a cough, *poor little sod,*
She says as if sod means someone
To be pitied, a tiny, compact, little
Man who does not understand why
He feels ill. She looks down at his red face
And brushes the blonde fringe back from his
Forehead. She shakes her head and drinks
A sip of wine from a flowered cup, she calls her
Evening tea as she gets her boys to bed.
The stairs above to their room seem
Endlessly steep, as if they are insurmountable,
Or, like a ladder to nowhere, they have no future
Destination. She does not want this.
*Poor little sod,* she says, coughing to herself
When the phone rings. If he could just get to sleep.

## Devotion to the Breath

I love you shallow.
I love you deep.
I love you in three parts and when you come in like a
lion
And leave like ice.

Clear and lucid as a thought,
And unfelt in the night and tightened
When I am nervous or frightened.

But you always are there
For me; in junior high, my lungs
Ached with the growth of adolescence
So painful the tissues rapidly growing in my body,
Three inches in height one year played havoc
On my chest.

I take you in as new and shiny and promisey,
And full of dope, and I let you go and ease
Out of all the old and ancient and dusty:
Long kept rooms full of fears and relatives
I do not know any more, the mustiness of old
Dreams lost before they were even a thought.

Mornings, you come in thick and heavy
And close to my skin, so heavy that coughs
And grumbles are necessary to bring you up and
over
And through my various allergies that have
Followed me through bed, cuddling my brain
And looking for a safe home when I was unaware.

Evenings you are quiet and sit still for the air
As it comes over my throat and whispers to me,
"Later, lover, later."

Without you I would not press through
Versions and divisions and passageways.

Breath, without you I would not be able to fly or
To swim in the world of language and gauge
The value of love and forgiveness.
I am dumb and easy and always here for you.
All my words are written between your punctuation.

## Sewing the Black

for Leslie Scalapino

Sewing the black silk irises
To pause, to sit, to listen to their
Cloth-ness or the tears of the silk
From worms we know not of nor
Ever discuss.

Turning the bulb turned
Inwards to the light inside
The outside of a part of us all,
She told us of thoughts
Deepened in their own
Water, then other randoms
Like houses that drew
Themselves to the surface.

Sitting, now, over the last bed
Of the one who made poetry
Into the conjoined pipes of a sad
Song we run through like a medieval
Maze of roses -- no, not roses.
Silk irises, black, the ones we are
Sewing now to say goodbye.

## Please

Written in response to the 2010 Gulf Oil Spill

May we not apologize for the earth's bleeding
Nor try stupidly to explain about cars and roads
And the endless highway of Americans needing
To drive. May we learn to get from place to place
More gracefully like the dolphins or the starfish.
May love carry the oil spill on its back and inside
Its sorrow. This day, I send to you, an address,
A blessing, dear fish and dolphins and sea creatures
Who understand the ways of man all too well.
A blessing more than we will ever --
And, yet, probably you know, I am sorry.
I love you. Please forgive us. These words, may they
Form clear oceans and blue silky water and safe
Havens to feed and nest and grow. By envisioning
this,
May there be a change in the molecules, a shift
In the palace. I am hoping to affect a miracle.
May you forgive us in this dear
Life of a planet. Please. We're sorry. We love you.

## The Morning Brittany Murphy Died

OK, I was in the UK,
Watching a kid's show
With our god babies and looking
At the first snow,
And my husband, the first
Seven months sober with a bum
Heart was every day a breath
Away from things being serious.

There was a special notice
And the story hit and last week
We'd watched *Ramen Girl*
And I hardly knew her even onscreen
Only my niece liked *Uptown Girl,*
But she was 28 or 32 and young
And diabetic and people
Said later she was on
Drugs.

She was in the bathroom for a half
An hour and no one knocked.
She had vomited and felt
Ill the night before.

And I was looking for signs
In my husband in Copenhagen
In the snow and in the Marlborough
Pub in Dedham where we sang
Karaoke to Sinatra's *New York,*
*New York.*

It was a Wednesday or a Thursday
Or maybe none of the above.
Christmas hopped up on us,
And we arrived with unwrapped
Presents, safe and fresh from airport
Security, having made it one
More time safely through the chest
Pats and the luggage take-aparts

And I remember Brittany Murphy
The celebrity, seemed so full of life
And so alive, and maybe it is the same
With someone old and maybe it is not,

But I cannot stop thinking of her.
Sick all on her own, trying to sit up
Maybe take a shower as if it were
Just another day and then failing
Miserably at pulling out of it.

## Somewhere Ahead a Man is Waiting

He wants to see you
But not to talk. He has other
Things on his mind: maybe mystery,
Maybe evil. There is a road
And a broken phone and the shell
Of an Enco gas station that closed
30 years ago. This man thinks
He knows what is best. This man
Imagines himself stronger than you
Are, with your lost face and open map
Of a mouth. He knows that the signs
Are all there but twisted like dead
Birds in a storm or a young American
Girl who knots her pony tail and then
Nibbles on the end. At the dusky
Café, this man is standing by himself
Having given up the right to ordinary
Talk with others long ago. He knows
What he wants now. He looks at his
Shoes. There is a song called by
Her name he used to know
Before he was alone. The bird
Of paradise only blooms when its roots
Are crowded. He steps forward.

## His Days

He rises, forty-six, in the same
Bed he grew up in, with his aging
Mother cooking breakfast,

His father, putting on white
Pants for the day's plastering
Where they will side by side

Smooth over walls and finish
Out new homes for families just
Moving in to start their lives.

He had twenty years, then ten
With children, building and stretching
His legs out on his own coffee table,

Taking the boys for ice cream,
And swimming and playing *Doctor
Who* games on the little computer.

He said he could not take
The arguments, the hostility, the change
In the marriage when they decided

To become parents. Like a wild animal,
He only knows he wants his food
And for life to be easy and not questioning

Of his motives. He imagines not much past
The day at hand for, to him, it will always
Be this way. There will be hearts and open

Arms and he will have his own way.
He shouldn't have to think or to consider
He wants his orange juice when he is thirsty.

He wants the luxury of skipping a meal.
Then, wonderful people sinking through
The wallpaper will serve him up a salty hot dog.

This is all he has known and he cannot understand
Otherwise. He needs to protect who he is:
The walls, swirling and thick and all around him.

## Birth

Not wanting to disturb the marriage,
my parents, or you: I enter backwards,
door through. The hallway strains
with my struggles: thick blooded pores enclose
my shoulders. If I can make it into the safety
of our bed without the angry walls screaming:
"Guilty, Jezebel, guilty,"
then I will be able to breathe.

In the living room, you my dear husband, my love,
you sleep: on the worn out sofa, like a child,
or a man who has given up. If my four legg'ed
shadow
can crawl past you all will be well.

The Bible and the headstones will rest
with me, buried deep in trampled grass:
it is where they belong. You never gave me
any trouble, dear husband, but you never gave me
any encouragement, either.

Do not utter a word, sleeping man;
this life we have is not so safe.

Forced into this world with cold forceps,
I now bring myself back. Husband, husband
who is asleep, holding the umbilical cord
like a rubber band: You keep tugging on my body,
making me small.

I am your boomerang who must return;
dragged back like Circe with sperm in my hair;
it is a planned breach un-birth.

And so, tonight after tonight, I will carry
my purse, hide my cigarettes, and pray
that you do not awaken.

Never staying born is a crucifix that weighs
and digs into my bloody shoulders;
it happens every time I leave him to go home.

Not wanting to disturb the marriage,
my parents, or you:
I enter backwards, door through.

## He Talks of Guns

He talks of guns and of protecting his
family of having the right not to wait
five days fifteen hours of the criminals
who will get guns anyway from places
we know not of  Dare never think about

He asks me if I've ever held
a weapon fired an arm felt the kick
of the bullet shooting out from beneath
my outstretched hands the target
a dream lost in the distance  I shake

my head with a No answer
He talks of how to fire his gun
and of how to choose between injuring
and killing and he mentions the NRA
and the Orange County gun show

last weekend when he came home empty
handed  He claims there is a weapon
of choice for the prey a man wants
a different gun for birds for snakes for deer
for rabbits  What about people I ask and he says

yes those are different too  I hear about
how he takes his gun with him
on trips in the car as if it were home
and he swears he hopes he will never use it
and yet it is still there itching in his glove

compartment  We talk of the election
and of voting for what we believe in
and I admire him just then for understanding
what he kills he eats and for not invariably
grabbing a package of hamburger from the market

I watch his mouth a smile of soft chiffon
Eyes clear and dark and Hispanic I know
he has been to a place I will never reach
knowing plenty about what he wants
in a woman  In the sights of his rifle

the eyes clear of a living being not of his own
kind  He knows what he can do with his bare
hands and then I think of his wife and I swear
he has a mistress and then I think of a friend
of mine  About how in art school he would hide

in the science building after class visiting
the rattlesnakes glaring terrified and then
rat ta ta tat tat ra ta ta tat  He struck
the glass with his fingers setting the snakes
off like traps  Running night after night
to them

## Leading me Towards Desperation

The pipe fitter
on my first job
explains how life
works

First off,
be jealous
not insecure

An insecure
lover
is doomed
Take a wife
In fact
take a few

just to teach yourself
Anything can be
gotten out of
Even taxes

he said and I believed
him because
I was young  just

escaped Vietnam
by a day
and I borrowed his
Winstons
and learned how to smoke

Even though
it would kill
my father
I practiced
inhaling the vapor
until I had made it
my own.

## Spitting Nails

I wondered why he stored them in his mouth.
Back home I begged my father to let me cross
the street to the library, two blocks away,
and, yet, in the desert, I carried a gun, killed

rabbits with my bare hands, cracking necks
to the sound of marbles clicking in my pocket.
In the desert I was fearless. Enough to now find
myself cabin roof-bound talking with the ex-sailor

who stored nails in his mouth. To go easily
into hard wood, you have to lubricate nails,
he said, serious. You have to spit into the hole
that you are about to make and then watch

how the nail drills into the heart of where
you want it. Spittle, white and foamy
as the ocean; I watched it extend from his mouth
onto the wood. If the boards are soft, he said,

pound down the end of the nail, blunt-like,
so it goes in slowly, without cleaving the board,
like a woman who has all night for you, like
a place you waited ten years to arrive at.

## Raising Butterflies

In half-secrets around his wife,
he and I spoke, my answers unheard,
the conversation otherwise harmless.

Without warning, his wife
seizes the mouthpiece, swinging
away from the face. It was, yes,

of course, expected, as all a part
of seeing him. A part of flying heedless
into the sun, melting. In a slightly mad

voice, his wife said: "Thank you,
If you were not here, I don't know
what I would. . ." I imagined the moths

and butterflies I had as a child, raised
from a mail order box, then later set free.
Those fragile wings and red flowers

soaked in sugar water. The friendship
I had given this man, the recent sex.
She offered dinner, to have me "over

to the house." As if face to face
would turn her into a strongbox.
As if she would be able to stop collapse

by contact with her hands, by extending
polite invitations, by flying without trust,

by continuing to love him long after I had
started to.

## Serving

Between the counter,
You and I work the swing
Shift. Food all night
Long, consuming us, as we
Fumble in our aprons
For pens. I can almost
Taste your smell.
Your face, like onion soup
I want. Long, hungry and
Awake, we pause together
Like cars at a stop sign.
Pause now, we are my hand
Near your trousers.
Take a breath, we are
Full of each other.
Full of your rummy skin.
Full of your slick hair.
Full of my calves.
Our hands now inside
The oily restaurant
Grill of you and me.
We press together
At the counter, serving
Coffee, writing checks.
We shift position,
Smoothing, changing
Places for side work,
Wiping off ketchup
Lids, filling sugar
Dispensers while looking

Down at our legs.
As if we are under
Water, I see the slow curls
Of sweat in your hair.
We have a fast drink
Later, after work,
Confirming the tips
As they are packed
In tall stacks of coins, inside
Paper cylinders ready
For the bank.

## At the Makeup Counter

Those days my own skin
So dewy, shiny, full of
Angles and blemishes
And fat and youth and hope.

I would sit my mother
Down in the try-on seat
At the Clinique counter
Of the Buffums on Pine.

Begging her to try the lilac
Shadow, the foundation
Promised to make her look
Suntan and gorgeous. For
This one day, removing her
From motherly comfort.

I was a kid, exploring Lip
Smackers and Clearasil
And Bonne Bell's Ten o Six.
I had no way of knowing
That my mother had not always
Looked this way, the creases

In her eyelids, the forehead
I traced like skirt pleats.
The large pores around her nose
From, she said, when she stepped
On a hornet's nest as a child.

Oh sure, the salesgirl
Tried to cover up things up
And make the skin glossy and bright
As Mary Jane's, tapping derma-powder
With a brush then shaking off the excess.

Making snowy peaks of Seventeen
Magazine perfection over my mother's
Cheekbones, the nicest part of her
Face, the area she always got compliments for.

She took to drinking
Hot milk at bedtime,
A comforting thought
After years of hating
The taste of the heavy
Texture of heated sweetness.

She took long baths
She could drown inside,
Her head near the edge
Going under to a place
Where the world seemed
Vulnerable and full of cotton.

After, she'd sit in her apartment
Looking below at what people
Did, walking by, laughing,
Throwing their words forward
When they spoke in earnest,
As if life was not an oyster but
A piece of candy that lasted all day

She consumed morning
Through night. Waking up
To noises that must be squelched,
Running in her dreams, then an awful
Surprise, waking suddenly from a jump,
A few moments before her heart crushed
Her upon the ground from a fall.

# Noon

## Photograph of My Mother as a Young Mother

She was looking
Shyly into the camera
When this photo was taken,
Standing uncomfortably
In a light colored suit with
Large shoulders and belted
Pockets at the hips.
Her right arm was straight,
But she was making a small
Fist as if she were anxious.
She smiles weakly, as someone
Unused to being photographed.
I am not sure
If this is Easter or another holiday.
Maybe 2 or 3, I am beside her,
Sticking out like a strong bite
Of wood, sturdy pageboy haircut,
Tomboy, earnest eyes. My own suit
Of a darker color, a short
Jacket with four large white buttons
Across the front, like an honor badge.
In a fashion popular at the time,
My mother has on her lucky silver
Earrings, this I know from the
Hint of sparkle at the side of her
Hair. This picture was taken during
Her red-headed period, when she
Channeled movie stars with their flipped
Soft waves about the face, bangs to one side.
Clearly 20 years after the fad died

Out. My mother is turning slightly
So as to face the camera,
As if to jump in and say, "Stop, don't
Take me in this outfit, just take the child,"
"Put the flowers in the background"
I have a lopsided bow in my hair, falling
Off, even with grandmother's
Bobby pins. The wooden slats
Of the house next door are barely showing
Behind the purple hydrangea bushes,
Which are larger than the Buick. Just out of
Camera range, the car, the future, my father,
And everything else.

## The Sculptor in his Fiftieth Year

Decided to have a child,
and to slink behind
buildings, listening for someone
to mention Marx.

Dealing indictments he reveled:
You have all deceived me;
you are all like empty stones.
Is there no one to trust,
but the ones who don't know
me yet?

The ones who don't know
about the life
cracks in the marble, the hunting
for a soul -- about Rodin
and the lost originals; the ones
who haven't heard of "The Kiss,"
and the two schools.

Artists don't act this way by sin
of sloth, by laziness;
he thought us as guilty as Brutus,
who stupidly listened to only one
voice echoing in the world,
echoing against an uncarved
esker.

Can you hear the sound
of the earth breaking
open like a fractured
rock when you tap your wife
on the shoulder?

Do the eyes of the ocean
follow your back so closely
that you keep turning
again and again to check,
to look at the very same still
water again and again?

And is your heart in a shoal,
the place with the least
water; and are you
floating ice, a floe
on a sea of landscape,
reaching for the alluvial
fan with which to revive yourself?

## Music Remembered from the Womb

Their music was played
long before father's coarse
face abraded my shoulder,
before he pushed my flesh.

Oh yes, I remember.
His hoarse notes driving
against mother's thin
legs.

The asking, the pleading
quietly in the room
around his body.
And then,

later, Mother's round
love and words
spelled out above
my head

as if I couldn't look
up to see the blue
sky, to understand
what I already knew.

Their twin grunts
at night, the hushes
during the day.
The closed doors

to transudation
magic. And I take
myself back to age ten,
to a Saturday.

And I press myself
against him because
that's what I do.

And his kiss takes
up my entire face.

And his dry lips
meet mine, in darkness
older than death.

And his hands fumble
with my skirt, pulling
apart cotton like curtains.

And I see what he
tells me is true.
The unmade wonder
of closed eyes, and the awful, awful
luck.

## Blessings in Disguise

In the guest house playing Mother
May I? catching their arms in my waist,
I was the child who wished her grandmother
Were in a circle, with her seven sisters,
Back in the room with the orange couch.

I am sure I am not the first daughter
Whose family did not see her married off,
Not the first to remember when she heard
The story of taking the train to the seaside.

I am certain I am not the first to want
A circle, continuous rather than a line,
In which to keep everyone in my life
Together, with only a beginning and a middle.

To anyone paying attention to what they think,
Or how they are, at holiday time, I wish
For no despair or depression, our lives frozen
Like a broken watch to the days when memory

Started. The eldest son, 13; mother in her
Yellow Jackie dress. My father taking
Grandmother to get pastrami sandwiches.
Photographs only show smiling faces,
And the way I spend my days, un-bound
Like loose knitting yarn.

Thoughts looking over me like freedom.
No one judging, no one writing down the heart-rules
We were supposed to remember.

## Why not the Irish?

My mother said, her red hair
And green eyes, glistening like fire.

It's always "The Portuguese!"
Your questions about
Immigration, what island
The family came from.

How to cook kale or salted
Fish, or malasadas. It's the questions,
About times in our lives
That your father would rather
Not remember, sweeping the porch

For his Uncle Manny, running away
From his great aunt Mary, crippled
With polio, who chased him under
The bed to deliver beatings.

The leather shoes three sizes
Too small that made your dad's toes
Curl up yellow. Why is it always
The Azores, the mystery of a dead
Language everyone wishes

To forget. No, he doesn't know
That song about his mother.
Why all this bothering of us, with
A Spanish surname. Your father
Is European. Not Hispanic.

Why is it that you cannot
Understand we do not want
This past. It's only a dialect.
No one reads it. English is what
You need. That's why your father
Goes to night school.

I don't understand your fascination
With Catholic school uniforms,
Your estranged cousins
In Dartmouth you never see them.

We moved away from the humidity,
And the church and scrimshaw
And the New Bedford streets filled
With dust.

To build a better life for you,
In the land of Disneyland not cranberries
Or lobster or whaling.

How about the Irish or the grandfather
Mixed into your blood. William,
We think he was born in Dublin.

Maybe we could talk
About your Grandmother
Who lived in French Canada.
Her stepfather was a plumber.
Let me tell you a story about the bobbins
At the thread factory.

## My Father

Collected Buddha
Only he called them Ho-ties for no
Reason I could figure. Somewhere
In his travels he was in the Navy
And had taken a fancy to them.

The statues were all over
The wooden shelves in the den:
Made of marble, soap, plastic, metal, copper.

A few stunning
Examples, some really awful.
The collection, a mixture
That plead no boundaries. Dad gathered
Them all, no matter what form.

No type was dear or special or valued.
A medicine Buddha, or praying
Or happy. Although many were cross-legged,
There were also those standing,
some holding their hands,

A few with open legs looking
As if they were ready to catch a heavy ball
The size of a human head.
Acquired in Germany, Russia,
Portugal, lost lands, never
Spoken of.

All throughout my childhood,
We rubbed their bellies
For good luck. I dusted and replaced.
Each statue a special aspect
Of the life my dad chose not to follow.

## Bully

I used to beat up little boys
as my mother's
Friends said, mostly Rex's mom
Josie at Bixby Park where the kids
Played in back of the outdoor stage.

The only girl on my block,
I was forced to deal with boys,
Boys who rode bikes and played
HORSE,
Who smelled like the pool
And wet dirt.

So, yeah, I get the squeezing
Meanness, the hard poking out of eyes.
I get the rush when the boy's head
Is rubbed against the grass,
Or pushed into the sand inside
The tunnel at the playground

The spitting on and rolling
In the leaves, jumping on them
From high up in the trees,
The making them take it
Back and eat sand and cry.

The admitting to me that girls
Are better and that
Given a choice they would rather
Play with me.

39

## Catholic

I should have been. My father
Was an altar boy, hiding
Under the bed to avoid
Early morning Masses said
In Portuguese.

I should have gone
To parochial school,
Wearing scratchy blue
And green plaid uniforms
Like my twelve cousins,
With little medals around
Their soft necks, getting
Gifts of rosary beads,
And bread with hard boiled eggs,
Pressed into the middle at Easter.

I should have been married
In the church by a priest
In a long white and golden robe.

My husband's
Family, also a bunch of
Ritualists, the faithful
Cultural believers,
Sharing a secret knowledge
Of the stations of the cross.
When to kneel and when
To utter, "Peace be with you."

I should have gotten
Baptized before I had
Time to consider the endless
Possibilities
Of a bright perfect world
Designed without a pattern.

## Daughter's Weakness

My father, he
Has not spoken

After we
Lost her, she, my
Mother

I was worried
For him
And wondered of lost
Years and time we could have

Spent
It was not my choice
By far, and yet

With no new
Pathways or suggestions
To follow, no questions

Time, it's gone by.
There it is. The distance
Of a new life

He hopes is what for,
One without
My mother or me.

A life. Inside it
Here he remembers

And then, just
Too easily, moves on,

Into other lives
Other happinesses.

## Firsts

It was not the first
Death that I remember.

It's not true what people say
About anything.

Hidden among the numbers
Of firsts and lasts that strike

Out and catch in your throat
Like a cough or a choking

Sensation that you cannot control.
That death catches you completely

During a time you imagined you had
Life handled what the great creator dished

Out. No, it's not the first birthday,
Or the first child or the first snow storm

Of the season. It's not the first boy
Who kisses you, or the manager who doesn't.

It's not the diagnosis or the illness,
Or the car wreck where the air

Bags hit you in the face. It is the
Relentless chance of unknowing

Of being incapable, of predicting
When the other shoe will drop
Out of the sky and end the world.

## Looking Back

They came to our house to buy
A used vehicle, with barely a $200
Down payment. We offered wine
And in those days we said too much
And didn't stop talking until the bottle
Was finished. We discussed names

And applauded their choices for Perfect
Diamond or Unique Gemstone or Ultra
Aqua Marine. Seconding the motion
That no one wants to have a name
Everyone else has and yet secretly
Wondering what was up.

They came to our house with a check
And a promise and what idiots we
Were, looking back. Us, asking the gender
Of the baby and talking about mixed races
And how strong the blood-line would be.
We confessed over dinner, me, dating a black

Man and him living with an Asian, others
Outside our race and that led to dogs and cats,
Horses, stud talk. About how much stronger
Mutts are than pure-breds. Look at the royal
Family with their big ears, we laughed.

Not meaning ill will just stupid. We had
Thought we were being inclusive, and kind
And chummy.

## Enterprise

Out in the dunks of Idaho
While I was waiting
To pick up my 75 Datsun at the garage,
I see a man who claimed he'd met Karl Marx.
In Russia, he said, Siberia.

He came to speak at a mechanics conference,
He said. There were purple ribbons and balloons
Decorating a stage of gray feathers.

In the middle of his talk he got out a sword
He said, and cut down the ribbons
In a brutal act of violence.

Eggplants, Marx voiced, Do not plant them,
They fool you, the sweet sweaty
Treasures. One day they are green
And shy, leafy even, then they pop!

He stabbed at a balloon.
The next day they are blown up
And taking over the garden.

The man in the garage was reading
A pornographic book while he told me about Marx,
With photos of large breasts, and I was young
With a short skirt I was protecting,

Trying to manage the hills where my car had
Just been stranded, then towed to.

On the back of the book
Was a black and white photo of Karl Marx,
Smiling, bearded, as if to say, Yes,
I have cut men in two, and I have no dispute
with the world.

## The Last Letter to my Mother

Was found in the laundry
Room, while sorting through papers,
An old packet of red-golden negatives.

The letter had a heart stamp
And was addressed in the all caps phase
Of my late twenties when I thought what I did

Was the most important story for the world
To read, and that my mother dwelled on me.
As evidence for the life she was unable to lead.

I had written it when she was going through
Alternating phases of sickness and chemo and
recovery.
She was, or had been, angry for my not being

Attentive enough. Not visiting as often as she had
Wanted. Of course, there was a new man.
But this one was different, not paraded through
A revolving door.

This one, she touched his beard and patted his face.
Later, I was grateful they had met.
At the time of the letter, I don't think I knew any
better.

It was probably a diatribe of reasons
For independence and or stories about work
schedules
I maybe explained I was trying to do my best,

And that she needed to let me grow up, even though
I already was.

## Living only with the Hands

In the room with a fire,
knotting as they go,
a mother's open fingers curl inwards,
crossover through strands
of untamed hair.

Loved from love by love

Women and pieces of ribbon
twist into vows, routines, scuttled air.
Memory by memory, the braids
link everything permanent, to everything temporary.

Loved from love by love

Cupping the strands which travel
side by side, brushing the flax,
combing through snarls
the mother calms her child.

In another room
a man eases his lover's flush
with a fingertip.

A man lays his vaulted head
on a woman's breasts.

A man attaches his hips
to firmament.

A man coils the web of vocabulary
behind his back.

Neck above neck
palm over palm,
knees between knees,
he covers her mouth with his words.

Was my sweater as a child
Perpetually backwards or sleeves
Turned up when they should be tucked
Inside. The rough wool next to my skin
Like a galaxy of planets.

It was rushing to get
Dressed for elementary school
And being constantly hungry
And running the mile and a half
At full speed with only 3 minutes
To inner space, stumbling on the open
Parts of the sidewalk
In the path of the Apollo rockets

It was leaving my sweater behind
On the bus, starting my period in bed
With my mother and getting a lecture
About growing up, showing me the
Pink book as if it were a special comet
Rotation only once every thousand years.

It was being cold inside and yet having
Warm hands like the three suns of Jupiter,
Cooling ice cream under the
Stove. Inside out was how I felt when
I flip flopped on the monkey bars
And each time I spun over the side,
My right toes leading the orbit,

As if with the instinct of a rough animal
My hands opened and down I fell
Into the sand below back on earth
In an openly even way.

## Wilson High

With flashlights held
In place by rubber bands
To our tall band helmets
We marched to *Star Wars*
We marched to *Rockford Files*
We marched to *The A Team.*
And we marched at our famous
Homecoming show
To *Everything's Coming up
Roses* where we made
The flowers spin around
As seen from the bleachers
When they dimmed the football
Stadium lights, and we marched
In formation and played
Our songs. That year the hit
Was *Rocky*, ten or twenty years
Past the movie's hype,
Then the *Wilson Fight Song*,
Notes we had written and balanced
On metal stakes attached to our
Instruments. Mr. Sandberg made us
Do it. Each year, inspiring the pattern
Of the roses, his crowning jewel.
For that, we traded weekend jazz
Festivals where we triumphed
And drank beer and roamed the hallways
Of nearby city motels as teens,
Our orange uniforms dancing in the sun.
But, in those days, the drummers ruled;

They brought down the house
When they raised their wooden sticks
And were, for us, the gods of all
The universe, their veins popping out
Of their red foreheads when they played
Eat my Shorts after the Bruins scored.

## Ah Ida

For my grandmother

Ah Ida you never caved
In well maybe once
In a moment
Of time you lost sight
Of what it meant
To carve out the truth.

Maybe once you caved
In and did the expected,
The thing you were
Not meant to do. Maybe you acted
Instead of lingering.
Perhaps, you jumped
Into a cage that did not have
Your name on it
Just wanting to strive ahead
In the Great Depression

Ah Ida, you held it all
For years, through the rituals
And the thoughts of what
Other people said about you
How things should
Be or should have been.

You braved the union
Politics and put up factory protestors
On your couch,
Holding court in the midst of newspapers

And oatmeal and domesticity

You roared your
Head in quiet ways, later.
The three wheeled bicycle.
The dungarees, the black clogs
With the red cherry
Buttons. You painted fences and befriended
Al, the mailman, the ragman who
Picked up rags and empty bottles
On Fridays. Sigh, the Pilipino house painter
Thinner than a water pipe.

You repaired fences
And canned turpentine alongside
Jam, pouring rusty nails
Into oily glass jars in the cellar

Even when it wasn't cool.
You wore a scarf tied like
What later became
Known as a do·rag
When your hair wasn't done.

## Poem Starting with a Line from Norman Dubie

Whatever it is that watches,
Has kept you from loneliness,
Has kept you from pain,
Has urged you, like an old radio show,
Out into the ocean in a storm
To sight the boat crashed (you are sure)
Alongside the lighthouse where you
Have holed up awaiting the dragnet,
Or the shadow or the green hornet
To find you before your ex partner
Digs up the treasury bills you buried
On the side of the cliff your husband
Sent his car over the side of. And, yes,
You are afraid of the whistles, the clock,
The phone that rings inconveniently,
At times when you least want to be reached.
Whatever it is that has kept you
On this path, this trail of running away,
Then, running into yourself
Like a promise made as a child, whatever that is
I am paying attention, and I am listening.

# Evening

## Sound is a Circle

for Miles Davis

He was.
Afraid of see,
and sleep and,
a kind of blue he was,
of sequined pants,
of white rimmed eyes,
of sketches in Spain.
He was,
filtered through
gated youth
and vocal chords.
He was
the discovery of ecstasy.

His sound is
a circle in the round;
his sound is
the need to keep moving;
his sound is
seven steps to heaven,
Water babies,
What it is. Decoy.

Tone tumbling thought.
Tension deciding the note.

He said,
I'm too vain to play anything

63

really bad
that I can help
not doing.

Nefertiti.
Quiet nights.
In a silent way.
The man with the horn.

So what.
I'm having the life
of my time.

Once, he said. Once,
my father gave me
a trumpet, he loved
my mother so    much.

## Not for Miles Davis

Don't turn around
For us the audience
You're the conductor
The creator the mixer of recreation

Turning cool jazz into blue
Music into techno pop
Interpreting Bird and then Michael
Jackson and even Cyndi Lauper
Into your kind of style.

Like Sinatra, you had nine
Lives, different creations
Of who we thought you were

Son of a dentist
Then brooding musician
Heroin addict and finally
Champion of young players

So don't listen to us
Don't turn around or start
Playing just because we want
You to twist that note
Into something we think
We want to understand.

## Lady Night

Her beads click. A savanna
dries up. She walks
back stage and waits.

We hear footsteps
and a door,
the blare of metal
touching metal touching
the syringe glass.

A worn-white
powder dissolves into
the hot spoon.

It purls a wayward
tone, one bar of music,
one vein worth saving.

She puts on
her gardenia, and a safety
pin punctures the tender
skin between nail and finger.

This pain is everything
she ever knew.
And everything was
that way except
for her pleasing face
and the way she liked to sing.

She talks low
now, intimately,
to someone she just
met, and laughs at the whisper
of noise.

So this is how it is,
how it is in this new crowd.
The velvet seats waiting
for the band to stick it hard
into a downbeat.

Her dealer around
the corner waiting in striped pants
cinched fast at the waist.

When the band boys step
away from the stage, she rubs
her wrist, parts
the curtains and remembers
the rent, the men, the love.

## In Second Person

(I must talk with things falling away)

To straighten your shoulders
In a way that rotates your arms forward
Into the socket. At first it will seem as if you
Are pushing out your chest in a comical
Way or as if you are against the wall
Of a firing squad.  Your palms will naturally
Roll forward and open like a flower petal
It is awkward but how things are meant to be
You've grown weary, bending over, hushing
At your desk. Bring the tops of your legs
To attention, feel your knees as they rise
Then straighten and push back your thighs
As if you are holding back a tidal wave
Or a mountain. Tuck your bottom under
Yourself like you aim to sit down but stop
Just before making the decision to do so.
Shrug your shoulders to open up your neck
Turn your chin a little upwards toward
A spot on the wall in front of you, pick
A focus point to stare at but not to sink into.
Spread all ten of your toes and really let your feet
Settle into the earth below as if they were
Homesteading. Now rise above any poses
Or postures or effort or sight or worries you
May have and listen. Just listen. Be quiet
And see what your body comes up with.

## How to Get Passionate

The Long Beach Ice Dogs parking lot
After the game, in his white Chevy
Truck, the rain outside, the windows
Fogged up as if we were in a hot cave
I heard people hitting the side of the truck
As the crowd left the stadium, tossing trash
In a can nearby, spiting and yelling for no reason
It was a secret and we didn't have much
Time. There were others waiting for us
At places we'd stopped calling home long
Ago. There was time, we knew, and less time
If we messed it up. It was a fine balance between
Lies and the truth; it was easy and hard at the
Same time. It was a pivot point in the history of us
Reducing the past and ignoring the future, we were
All that was there, with the popcorn and the game
And everyone else in our loves fading into the
scoreboard
Outside the cave that we were loathe to enter.

## So it Was

So it was
Not an affair,
No one cheated
Or lied quietly as a returning
Lover turned away the covers.

It was purses
Left in one room,
The guests
In another. It was not drugs
or being strung out.

It was shopping
And a confession
Before the wedding,

A theme of blue and gold
And bright like peacock feathers,
The cake samples, already tasted

Courses selected, tents
measured. The white
Sleeveless dress of a lifetime
Bought on an installment plan.

Already paid for by Christmas
Last. It was not a fight over the budget
Or the poodle dog.

No one said ill words or threw furniture.
Instead it was
An excess of looping
Into oneself like a small child hiding underneath
A car seat so no one could find her.

## Jules

For Julie Streapy

I saw her once, years ago
In Beverly Hills, at a café.
Long after we'd lost touch.
She seemed thin, rich, with people
Who looked as if they wanted nothing
To do with me. Back in the 80's
We'd been roommates, driving each other
Insane in a beach-front apartment
In Seal, the kind on Electric Avenue
That flooded every day the sky
Looked like it would rain.
We had no furniture and moved in
Not knowing what we would need.
We were young and naïve and hopeful.
Not realizing we needed a fridge,
Or heat or even knowing how to phone
The electric company. In those days
There was a revolving door of boyfriends,
Wacky mango diets, blender margaritas,
And waitressing jobs. It was a time
Spent before we had to grow up. A time
After high school when we didn't know
It yet, but we were looking for ourselves
And who we thought we would turn
Into.  It was Tainted Love and The Doors
And going to the Roxy and The Whiskey
And standing around backstage to catch
A glimpse of Billy Zoom, Exene and The Plugs

At Starwood. It was counting change
In a large mason jar and locking
The landlord out when he tried
To come in and yell at us for taking
Too many showers. It was breaking
In through the levered glass windows
That are illegal now when we forgot
Our keys and wanted back inside.

## Soap Operas

There were the couches; the dreams
Steps down from the college entry way,
Full of weddings and seedy pasts and rape.

The debut characters all of us cheered
Against when they were onscreen.
The tea parties and gossip, the hospital scenes.

And, though I didn't actually
Follow the storyline, I knew of a young
Demi Moore as a throaty reporter
Like a main stay on a sail boat, sure to rise.

It was only that one year I was caught
In the web of daytime television.
At a school where you could legally smoke.

Enjoying the habit, I appreciated
The possibilities. Viewing *General Hospital*
In the glory days of Luke and Laura.

Watching my days out as a waitress,
Just to see what it would feel like to be alive,
Between growing up and staying small.
And always, those big screen televisions
Attached to the ceiling above, calling to me.

## Tana's 90th Birthday Present

For mom-Tana

We are all smiling
It's June 18th
1938.

Your Aunt Jean,
Me and the other Tana
from Massachusetts.

Rosemary said,
When she sent the photo
That she thought
It was a celebration.

Maybe a wedding,
Or a baby shower.

When I saw the date
I knew.

It was my graduation
From high school.

My parents had thrown me
A party.
I was 18.
I was young and happy

I had not met Joe
Yet or tasted peaches.

We'd not gotten married.

Of course, later that same
Year, Tana had her nuptials,
And then Jean after her,

But that day
Was mine.

## The Las Vegas Tunnels

Black widow spiders
Abound in the wet darkness

Under Las Vegas,
The unemployed and the addicted

Run schemes during the day light.
A credit hustle, picking up slot machine

Credits and found chips to buy food.
Their beds held just above the impending

Flash floods. The ever-present damp cement,
A cool testament that they are not just camping out.

Plastic milk crates hold books and a special
Rigged shower made from a water dispenser

Echo this temporary life. Temporary, like Vegas
itself.
Lucky some days, not so lucky other days.

Amid the gold and glitter, the city seems
To take more than it gives, everywhere are signs

Of impermanence, everyone here is a visitor of sorts
There are no natives, no real locals. Even the tanned

Well-seasoned cocktail waitresses came from somewhere
Else. A good storm could flood the tunnels, caving into a roaring

River in a matter of seconds with rain. Or, a roll of the dice
Could give the 700 underground residents another twenty years.

## Chopin

Into the wide world, with no very clearly
defined aim, forever-- Jachimecki

One without
The other,
Says Delacroix,
Both will come together.

Find the mirror
Of a mirror.

Wait for the sound
Of a nightingale's full round
note.

A waltz in A-flat,
Uncertain where the music
Will settle
For good

A tormented heart,
One that dared not
Inform him
No one else was listening.

Sonata,
Mazurka, waltz, nocturne, étude,
Impromptu and prélude,
The piano begins.

Blue rings out,
Sounding in the ears,
Cloud in his lungs.

Uncertain is the shape
Of romance.
Sketching and observation
Finds
Nothing but moonlight.

Mediterranean and dawn are
Melodies
Written from life.

## More Polish than Poland

Light-hands,
Embark
Then stop.

He dreams of
Where he died many
Times in a French
Novel.

Colors begin
Like a quickening.

Erotic transports,
Modulations,
Clouds taking on fantastic shapes.

Chopin is
playing Polish
Folk music.

The piano,
A solo instrument.

## The Last 40 Years

Inspired by Jiri Stransky, Prague, 1993

In
the moment
I have done nothing,
many things, at once, together.
Only those people called
dissidents believe in precise
quotations, altered photography, fevered
questioning.
In captivity, the first things we draft are lyrics,
motionless, from a world that is no longer true,
formed by memory, not stones. Knowing
every minute where the word "enemy"
is, we move freely through sentences,
words shift through our heads
like followed commands.
When we have no chance
to write, we talk, holding
disagreement beneath our tongues,
exhausting stories, generations depleted
by a simple change of name.
In the moment I have done nothing, many
things, at once, together.
With the rhythm of tiny, little
thoughts, all our own, we decide
to continue, to dig the Soviet's uranium.
Our bodies tell us to drink an odd amount
of tea. Our humor is only lost
over torture. We never write about food.

After three days in a water cell,
like children burying dead animals,
we hide manuscripts under floorboards.
Such was our life.
Now, with no official enemy, we must
swallow that crossing of the Rubicon,
that other bank. Siberia, Russia, Germany.
We stumble together like a crumbling wall.
In the moment I have
done nothing, many things.

## The Argument

In this alley, I cannot carry out my usual
Threats. Angry, already knowing what I need,
I throw our passports at the building,
As if there were snakes.

In the madness of rage, we don't even recognize
each other's clothing, touching each other
As if we were blind.

Ahead, the illuminated windows of a church.
In this, each other. Now. Like birds' eyes,
The street lamps follow us.

Anger, we nod into deeper states
Of bewilderment. We wander through lingo,
As lost as this place

With its unmarked streets. Prague makes us snap,
react oddly, like voices firing from guns.
Looking for a place to sit down, I go unnoticed,

as if I were veiled. I condemn you, battling
The crowds in Wenchelas Square. We try,
To imagine our future. Lies adhering to white cloth.

In this city, we curse; my fists hit your arm.
Long across the way, road workers stare
and young children retreat from the Consulate.

Stumbling like drunks through commotion,
We follow after our own escape. Around a large
stone,
a bestial sound greets us. Purple chalk marks of
triangles

On children's hands catch my eye. What does it
mean?
Like someone in trouble, you offer to kill
for me. I feel the cold wall; I'm pressed against it

Like frozen water. We wish, for a moment,
we liked resistance. We wished we needed a cause
to believe in. In this city we keep trying. We hear
The words of hymns on fire.
In this city, we are the Ugly Americans.
As if I were a mad women, or someone to give
A wide berth to, you slap my face, an action
you would never take back home in the states.

## Manhattan

She had already had him
On her mind, the financial
Analyst she could not stop
Talking about at the burger joint
In Mid-town, in front of the Mitzvah
Tank on the way to the harbour and
Even when we were buying fake Prada
Purses on Mulberry Street.

She had already had him
On her mind when she insisted on
Breakfast at Tiffany's for expensive
Cufflinks, with the famous logo, clutched
Secretly in her palm as her boy children
Begged for FAO Schwartz and Night
At the Museum with Dexter and Dum Dum.

She had already had him
On her mind when she walked up the stairs
After the second elevator on the Empire
State Building and looked through the large
V shaped openings of the metal fence
At the End Iron, Met Life and Chrysler buildings
No longer housed by companies for which
They were named.

She had already had him
On her mind when her husband snapped
A photo of her with a rush of emotion

As her chin turned down against the wind
As if she were kissing someone else.

She had already had him
On her mind when our two families
Had lunch at Rockefeller Center, watching
The ice skaters circle the frozen ring.

She had already had him
On her mind when her boys' father, exasperated
Stood up and said, "Well, there's nothing to see
Here, is there?" He threw his tray and the silverware
Hit the floor and the plates bounced like
A heart too weightless to begin with, empty
Plates too light to even do a decent job of breaking.

## The Story of the Ten Blackbirds

Blended at times into
The three little pigs
Or the Catholic Saints.

Aunt Flossie ripped
Pieces of newspaper
Or envelopes into ten

Roundish pieces
Three of her fingers were lost
Partially in an accident

To the cotton mills of
French Canada when she
Was a child

The index, cut at the nail
The thumb in half,
And her first lost at the joint.

She licked each piece
Of paper and attached
Them dampened to

The whole and the partial
Digits. This little blackbird
She said, went to market

As she whirled her hands

In the air then quickly behind
Her back. Miraculously one

Blackbird vanished
This little bird was fat
And forgot to pray to St Anthony

Her hands shook and
Another flew away
On and on it went as I watched

Rapt, kneeling at her feet
Holding onto her legs, astonished
At her magic tricks. Horrified

By her fingers. With a whirl of her
Tongue and a great fluttering
All ten blackbirds returned

Home to all ten fingers that
Auntie Flossie held up for me
To inspect, the sweaty bits of paper.

# Victory

Everyone called her Vicki,
And it was more normal,
And she thought it was a way
To fit in, especially since
She worked at Honolulu Council.

But, her real name,
The one she was christened
With and the word her parents
Wrote in hard pencil on the
Birth certificate

Was a talisman
For the end
Of World War II,
A charm
For the first of the boomer
Babies, one of the lucky

Children brought into the world
During a brief time of peace.

She and her husband loved
Skiing, and she made
Invitations and birth
Announcements gently
By hand, like the one for my
Friend April's son nine years ago.

Her real name was not Vicki,
Instead, she was crowned
For strength, delivered
In compassionate joy.
Birthed into what her
Parents thought
Would be an easier life,

A life, filled with inventions
And flying and space travel
And gadgets and, yes, even
Something called the twenty-first century.

## Acknowledgments

Grateful acknowledgment is extended to the following publications in which these poems (or earlier versions) first appeared:

*Caprice* "Birth"
*Chant de la Sirene* "Sewing the Black"
*Folio* "Enterprise"
*Footsteps: A Journal of Contemporary Writing* "Serving"
*Interim* "Raising Butterflies"
*International Poetry Review* "The Last 40 Years" "The Argument" "Directions"
*Karamu* "Music Remembered from the Womb"
*New Verse News* "The Las Vegas Tunnels"
*Nimrod* "Leading me to Desperation"
*Poets and Artists* "Manhattan"
*Room of One's Own* "Lady Night," "Music Remembered from the Womb"
*Rufous City Review* "His Hand on Her Black Pants"
*Salt River Review* "Somewhere Ahead a Man is Waiting"
*Seattle Review* "The Sculptor in His Fiftieth Year"
*Small Pond* "Living Only With the Hands"
*State of Emergency* (Poets respond to the BP Gulf Crisis) "Please"
*The Southern California Anthology* "He Talks of Guns"
*Witness* "Spitting Nails"
*Xavier Review* "Sound is a Circle"

Special grateful thanks go out to the National Endowment for the Arts; the California Arts Council; the Corporation of Yaddo; Jentel; Fundación Valparaíso in Mojacar, Spain; Milkwood in Cesky Krumlov, CZ and the Barbara Deming Foundation (Money for Women) for their support and encouragement—especially when I most needed it. "Chopin" and "More Polish than Poland" are included in the anthology *Chopin with Cherries* (Moonrise Press).

## About the Author

Millicent Borges Accardi, a Portuguese-American poet, has received literary fellowships from the National Endowment for the arts (NEA), the California Arts Council, Barbara Deming, and the Formby Fellowship (Special Collections Library at Texas Tech). Her chapbook, *Woman on a Shaky Bridge* is with Finishing Line Press. Residencies include Yaddo, Jentel, Vermont Studio, Fundación Valparaíso in Mojacar and Milkwood in Cesky Krumlov.

Breinigsville, PA USA
05 January 2011
252753BV00002B/55/P